I feel...

 happy
 calm
 sad
 angry
 worried
 confident

 scared
 surprised
 disgusted
 unsure
 excited
 embarrassed

 panicked
 focused
 disappointed
 silly
 friendly
 jealous

 bored
 muddled
 tired
 unwell
 hungry
 hot or cold

How do I say "I feel sad" in Makaton?

I feel

Take one hand with your thumb and middle finger pointing to your face and lift your hand up and say, "I feel".

sad.

With a sad look on your face, place one hand in front of your nose and move it downwards and say, "sad".

ISBN 978-1-78270-691-5

Copyright © Channon Gray

All rights reserved. No part of this publication may be reproduced or utilised in any form or by any means electronic or mechanical, including photocopying, recording, or by any information storage and retrieval system now known or hereafter invented, without the prior written permission of the publisher and copyright holder.

No part of this book may be used or reproduced in any manner for the purpose of training artificial intelligence technologies or systems. In accordance with Article 4(3) of the DSM Directive 2019/790, Award Publications limited expressly reserves this work from the text and data mining exception.

First published 2026

Published by Award Publications limited
The Old Riding School, Welbeck, Worksop, S80 3LR

awardpublications @award.books
www.awardpublications.co.uk

25-1206 1

Printed in China

All About
Sad Scribble

Written and illustrated by
Channon Gray

award

Sadness is gloomy and slow.

It is a feeling that takes over your body from head to toe.

Sob, sob! I am Sad Scribble.

It's okay to feel sad —

though it might surprise us.

BIG feelings, like sadness,

come in all shapes and sizes.

Sadness happens when we do less of the things we enjoy.

And we might cry,

when we feel that
we're failing,

no matter how hard we try.

It can feel like a rain cloud pausing over our heads,

Being sad feels and looks different for everyone!

It might make you want to cry, or hide or avoid having fun!

Feeling sad can help us to let go of experiences that are **BIG** and **heavy.**

When we feel sad, we have low energy.

Ahh! I am Calm Scribble.

We stop doing things that matter to us
and can feel like we are losing our identity.

To help us feel better, we must remember who supports us.

Let's ask for help! I am Ask Scribble.

Help!

Five trusted grown-ups I can talk about my BIG feelings to are...

When we feel sad, we should talk to those people we trust.

We value things that we think are important and helpful.

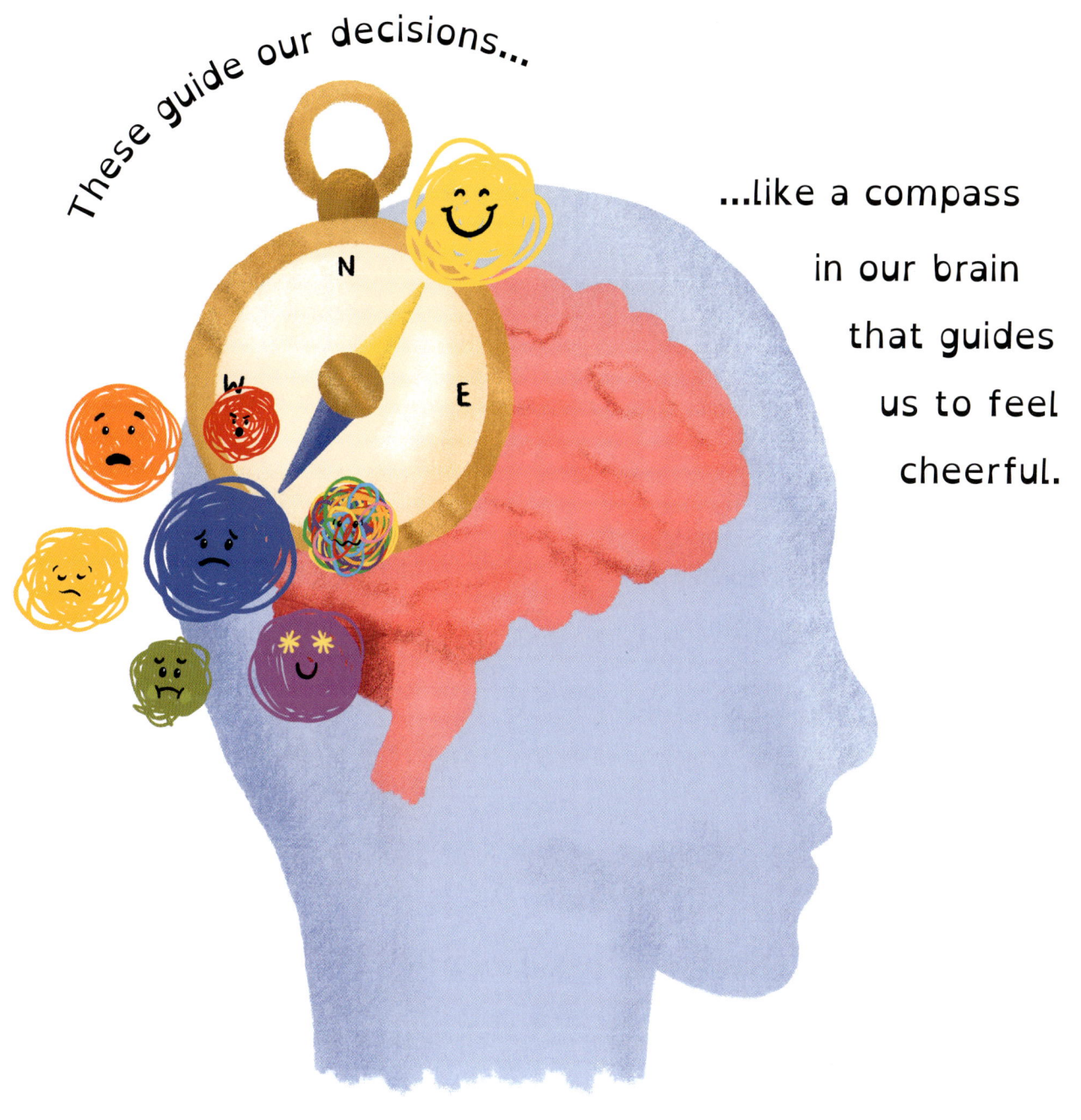

You may value spending time with family,

playing with friends

or getting stuck into hobbies

you find fun...

Ahem! I am Confident Scribble.

...being kind,

moving your body

or getting things done.

Aww! I am Kind Scribble.

What do you value?
What makes you smile?

Wahoo! I am Happy Scribble.

Grab some paper and a pencil. Let's write down what you value and then think for a while.

When we feel sad, we stop doing things that we normally like and this makes us feel unhappy.

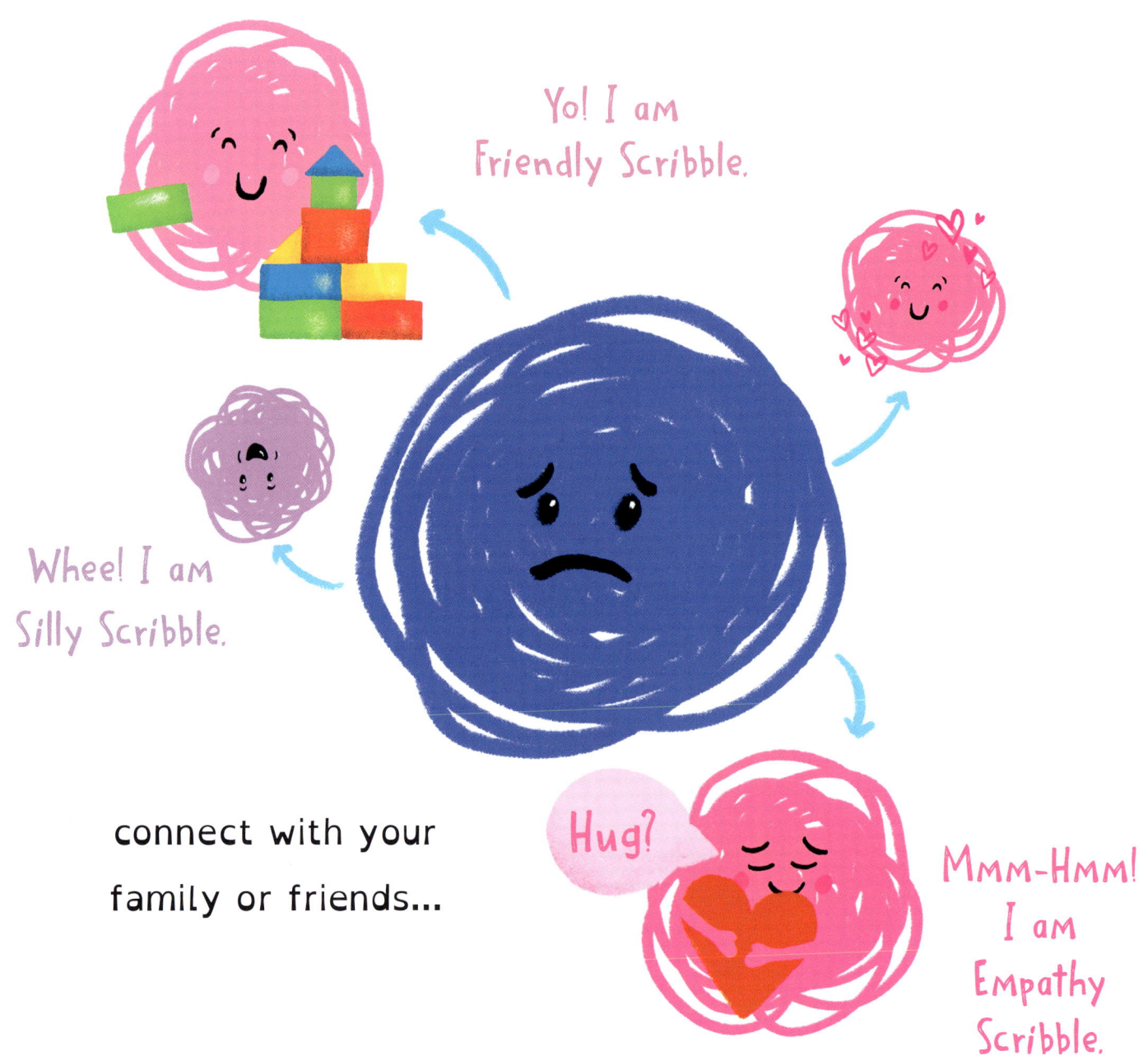

...ask for a hug

or chat about your sad feelings.

That is how the sadness can mend.

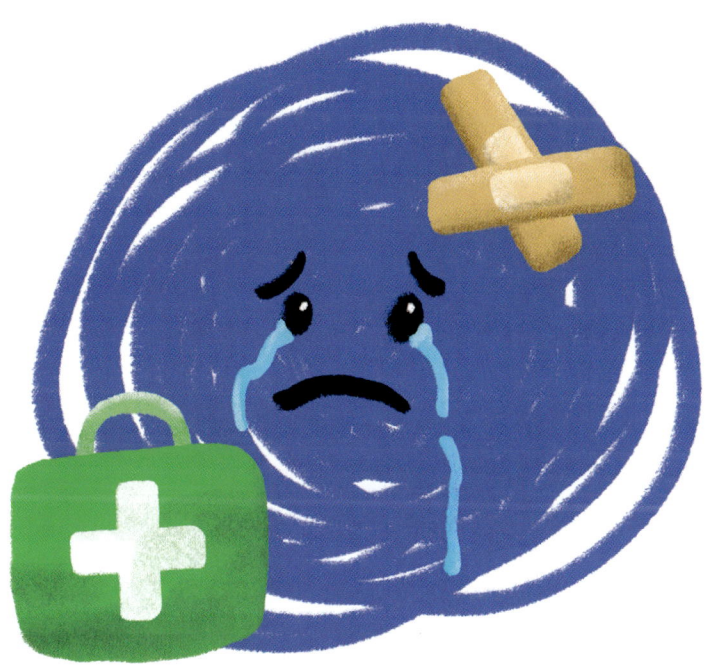

If we feel lonely, disappointed or defeated...

Hmmph! I am Lonely Scribble.

I need to eat well!

...looking after our bodies is a good way to feel treated.

I need to get more sleep!

Zzzz! I am Tired Scribble.

...you must remember to keep doing what makes you feel calm, happy and brighter.

Sadness might make us feel lost
like we're searching for a signpost,

but it can guide us to find out
what matters to us most.

Although being sad
can make us feel weak...

Sad Scribble Activities

Design your own 'Rain Cloud' by writing the things that make you feel sad on the raindrops. Imagine them falling away.

Pretend you are a weather reporter and share a weather forecast for a sad day and another for a hopeful day.

Create a 'Sadness to Gladness Map'. Using a big sheet of paper, draw a path and show the steps you take to feel happier.

The Scribbles Crew love to see your creations! Ask your grown-ups to share them on social media using #TheScribblesCrew

Scan the QR code on the back cover for more great Scribbles Crew activities, sing-along songs and teaching resources specially created by The Exciting Teacher.

www.thescribblescrew.com